Mercy for the Forsaken

by

Darla Scheuch Kellar

authorHOUSE®

AuthorHouse™
1663 Liberty Drive, Suite 200
Bloomington, IN 47403
www.authorhouse.com
Phone: 1-800-839-8640

This book is a work of non-fiction. Unless otherwise noted, the author and the publisher make no explicit guarantees as to the accuracy of

First published by AuthorHouse 10/22/2007

ISBN: 978-1-4343-3909-6 (e)
ISBN: 978-1-4343-3910-2 (sc)

Library of Congress Control Number: 2007906943

Printed in the United States of America
Bloomington, Indiana

This book is printed on acid-free paper.

The author's proceeds from this book will go to "The Remembering Tommy" foundation to benefit America's homeless.

* Special Thanks *

Tommy's family is gratefully indebted to Pastor Michael Vasquez, his wife Barbara, and The Children of The Shepherd Church in Hollywood, California, for all their aid and compassion shown to Tommy and others like him, homeless.

Also any others who gave food, shelter, medical aid, or kindness to him, "Thank You From Our Hearts!"

The author's proceeds from this book will go to "The Remembering Tommy" foundation to benefit America's homeless.

A special thank you to my husband, Bill for his support in making this book possible; also thanks to my girls Rene', Amanda, and Jesse for all their help.

Dedicated to the memory of
Tommy Edward Scheuch
Beloved brother of Johnny, Darla, Mark, and Becky

July 27, 1955 – September 15, 2005

Author's Note

My brother Tommy lived most of his adult life homeless and addicted to alcohol. His death raised many questions of "Why?" Why had he turned to alcohol having been raised in an alcohol-free home? He was smart, handsome, young, very likeable, and a hard worker. Most of all, why wasn't he able to overcome an abusive childhood and fit into society?

To answer these questions it was necessary to plow through the early memories of our childhood and go back in time. Bones of our past that were long ago buried had to be unearthed and exposed to the light of new sight, the hindsight of age and with it a better understanding and wisdom.

It wasn't my intention to write a "Daddy dearest" manuscript but in order to place the blame with its rightful owner, it was necessary to expose our father's abuse.

Abuse was indeed the hypothetical bullet that pierced Tommy's heart and crippled his spirit. I simply shined a light on the hands of the person that held the smoking gun.

Like many abused children, Tommy loved and looked up to his abusive father, viewing Daddy as the perfect man no other could compare to.

Placing Daddy on top a pedestal left Tommy to carry the burden of blame on his own back. The abuse he suffered became his own fault in his mind. He grew up believing he was stupid, worthless, and could never be as good as others. Deserving the slap at three years old, which slammed him into the floor because his shoes were on the wrong feet. Blind sided, he never really saw Daddy for who he was, a bully and coward … I did.

A sister should never have to "write" a wrong done to her brother but if it can help other Tommies then the pen in my hand becomes an uplifted sword, a sword to do battle against child abuse, homelessness, and alcoholism.

In January 2007, California passed a "NO SPANKING" law for children under the age of three. I would like to see all of our states do the same. The message California has sent to the rest of the world is that it's state cares about children.

Tommy survived brutal beatings that began when he was a toddler. As he aged his beatings grew progressively worse. The fact that he didn't die of a blood clot from severe bruising makes his life one of miraculous and divine intervention.

Since childhood the question, "Why didn't God help us?" burned unanswered in my heart. It would take me a lifetime to understand that while He wouldn't take away Daddy's free will, His hand was always holding onto ours. All scripture was taken from the King James version of the Holy Bible.

Led by the beautiful voice of Celine Dion lifting God in song (Celine Dion, "These Are Special Times") helped me find the courage to revisit times from my past filled with darkness and despair. She sang, I wrote. "Thank You, Celine."

This manuscript is my song to humanity. In its pages beats a rhythm of hope that through "Mercy For The Forsaken," other Tommies will be helped and mercy find them before they are lost to the streets of despair, leaving their family and loved ones to ask, "Why?"

Darla Scheuch Kellar

And whosoever shall offend one of these little ones that believe in Me, it is better for him that a millstone were hanged about his neck and he were cast into the sea.

Mark 9:42

Tommy age 17

Chapter 1

Homeless

I've heard what doesn't kill us makes us stronger but that isn't always true. Some wounds aren't visible to human sight. Like those that lay buried deep beneath the skin. Wounds that never fade away unlike bruises.

Sometimes hurtful words and treatment brand young, tender hearts with a fire iron that burns a lifetime, slowly eating away layers of hope until only ashes of despair are all that's left.

How much of our lives is fate and how much is free will? Where does one end and the other begin? Can free will change fate?

God gives us free will and democracy gives us freedom. Oppression and tyranny can take freedom until it's just a word whispered on the lips of a prayer. Parental abuse of power can take all of a child's freedom except the little crumbs called thoughts and beliefs kept hidden and guarded. It can do worse than take freedom, it can also distort, cripple, maim, and even kill a human spirit without mercy.

Tommy and I grew up side by side. Our lives entwined by the same threads and yet we wove different tapestries. His cries will always echo through my heart, prisoners of my memory.

I ask myself where and when did his pain become the definer of his destiny?

Addiction to alcohol kept him locked into homelessness but it was the child abuse that weakened his soul to addiction. He was beaten down too many times to stand tall and proud. So he did the only thing he could, he became one of society's lowest class … the homeless.

Rich in humility, poor in spirit, and drunk as often as possible. His shame is on the man we called "Daddy."

The bonds that pulled us together were more than just family or our ages. His treatment and pain linked us, but love was the super glue that fused us forever to each other. It was empathy for Tommy's treatment that filled me with a desire for righteous justice. His pain came from Daddy, mine came from witnessing his and being helpless to stop the abuse.

By the age of five, I had already seen evil, heard evil, and from repeating Daddy's cuss words, spoken evil. I felt the power of forbidden words to all in our home but the lord and master himself, Daddy. I learned his golden rule that same day, "Do as I say, not as I do."

When I was too young to know my age, I remember asking, "Mommy, did Daddy hurt our baby?" Tommy had just been beaten with Daddy's leather belt. I may have been three and Tommy one and a half. There would be many more beatings to come.

By the age of four and a half. Tommy already had all the makings for a future serial killer. What kept him from becoming one? I believe it was his heart.

He couldn't pronounce my name Darla, so it came out as Dardee. One summer day while we were outside playing, he held a big stick and began beating a fence post. He was re-enacting his own abusive beatings on the fence post with such force that his little face became distorted and twisted. His face was mirroring what he saw in Daddy's when he was beaten.

At six years old, I knew where his behavior was coming from and why. It disturbed me so much, I took off running for the house to tell Momma he was doing it again.

Side by side we stood with our bare feet in summer grass, looking up at a star-filled night sky, hoping to glimpse a peek at God's face.

The years ahead were those that would embed seeds into the fabric of our hearts and minds. Seeds that would grow and shape us into what we would be when we grew up. The seeds were of self-worth, self-confidence, and self-esteem. Ours were crushed beneath Daddy's boots.

In our last conversation we had, Tommy said, "I guess we did the best we could with what we had."

I wish his eyes had never beheld the madness of evil or his heart felt its touch.

Daddy kept his promise to beat Tommy within an inch of his life. Tommy lived and his bruises healed. But he would never take a breath as an adult without a broken spirit. By the time he was a grown man his spirit was so fractured, it resembled a kaleidoscope mirroring millions of a child's tears … his.

All the pain, rejection, and suffering he endured became his shame. It was a Pandora's box that he kept tightly shut. Alcohol eased the weight of the box for him.

My heart is filled with as many questions as there are stars in the sky. Why did he fill his stomach with alcohol until it poisoned his body? Why did he need it more than food, water, or air? I know alcohol ended his life, but the real monster came from his childhood and it wasn't hidden beneath his bed or in a closet.

Why did Tommy give such a high seat in his heart to Daddy? A seat unjustly occupied. How could he forgive the lord and master of his pain and torment? May our father be given the same mercy he gave to a helpless child. Tommy's soul was made of finer dust, now that's all we have left of him ... dust.

Tommy never held a grudge toward anyone. He loved and forgave. That's what made him so special to all who knew him and to God, who called him home, his heart.

Based on my memories and time spent with him, this is Tommy's story, an unvarnished sad reminder to this world that "Tommies" are in it with us. We can look the other way in disgust or we can feel compassion for the forsaken and show mercy.

But by the grace of God, there go I.

Chapter 2

Hunger

Autumn of 2005 will always be remembered as bittersweet by me. A celebration with the birth of my granddaughter, Faith. And mourning with the loss of my brother, Tommy. His death awakened me to the plight of the homeless and the reasons behind his life huddled in with humanity's unwanted homeless on the streets of America.

When Momma went to the hospital to have her third baby she was given a shot of sodium pentothal, sparing her from the pain of childbirth. Born the third of five kids, he was named Tommy Edward after our father.

Daddy never considered it an honor nor Tommy a blessing. A thought that had dug its heels into his mind sank deeper and deeper until it was swallowed by a quicksand of madness.

The thought corroded his heart against an innocent baby ….

Tommy. Rejected as being flesh of his flesh, just the sight of Tommy made the thought in his brain pulsate with demonic anger.

It was July 27, 1955, the first day of Tommy's life and the beginning of his pain. The only Bible Scripture I remember Daddy quoting was: Spare the rod and spoil the child (Proverbs 13:24). That verse became his creed in raising us kids. He used God's word to justify the abusive whippings inflicted by him. The verse said rod, not rods.

Tommy didn't get spankings, he got whippings, hard slaps to his face and head as well as word abuse. He grew up being referred to as "S.O.B." and "little bastard."

Lazy wasn't a part of his life. He worked hard cutting firewood and fenceposts, digging holes, shoveling snow, and doing farming and whatever he was told.

Every nasty job that came up was given to Tommy. When he was six years old we lived in the mountains of Romney, West Virginia. Our home was a two-story, no frills, no plumbing, old house heated by a woodstove. In the winter it was so cold that our oldest brother, Johnny, caught his pajamas on fire several times from standing too close to the woodstove while trying to get warm.

Daddy wasn't employed and Momma was pregnant with our little sister. That winter snow kept falling, piling up until between the deep snow, wind, and cold it was a blizzard.

Tommy was sent outside into the deep snow to empty our chamber pot. Daddy stood watching at a window because he knew Tommy would slip and fall. That's exactly what happened and when he fell he was covered by the contents of the pot.

Winter overstayed its welcome and March came roaring in like a lion. Momma had to be taken to the main road with the help of a neighbor's farm tractor pulling Daddy's car. She made it to the hospital and with spring came our new baby sister, Rebecca. Becky for short.

Our family had grown to five kids.

Two months later our world was rocked while we were at school when the fire alarm sounded. Several older students were volunteers of the fire department. Kids came running up to me saying it was our house that was on fire.

On the bus ride home I sat next to a window. The bus seemed to pass our driveway in slow motion, never stopping. My eyes locked onto the blackened spot where our house had stood that morning. Now, all that remained were cinders and ashes. Dreamlike, I stared at the remains of what had been our home. The cold house had at last gotten warm.

The bus driver let us off at our neighbor's. Together Johnny, me, and Tommy walked the long driveway in silence. Our neighbor told us Daddy, Momma, Mark, and Becky were at our grandmother's in Mt. Rainier, Maryland, and would come soon to pick us up.

I learned that day at eight years old what matters most in life, family. Even though all my dolls had melted away like the snow and our home was gone, I still had a real live baby doll … my two-month-old sister, Becky!

Out of the fire's ashes rose a monster that chased me the rest of my childhood. A fear of being orphaned or separated from my brothers and sister filled me with anxiety ignited by the fire. I worried how Johnny and me would keep us kids all together if anything happened to Daddy and Momma.

I remembered having been separated once in the past and any thoughts of it happening again drove me to tears. No one would take all five of us kids. How would we stay together?

The fire's origins were questionable enough that Daddy had to go to court over it. Arson couldn't be proven. He'd covered his tracks well. It was the second home we had lost to fire. I wondered if the first one was practice for the second.

Because Daddy was unemployed so often, he was slick at finding houses that were rent-free. These were owned by elderly widows who no longer wanted to live so far out in the country. On the promises of caretaker, the landowner welcomed tenants who would do repairs, upkeep, and oversee their property.

One of these houses was a large pre-Civil War mansion. The house had four fireplaces and more rooms than we could use. It also had a horse and a pony!

There was a large corncrib attached to the barn filled with ears of feed corn. With Tommy's help, I would climb up to the door, then given a shove by him, I'd tumble into the corn. I would get corn to feed to the pony and catch blackbirds!

Johnny, me, and Tommy all had the chicken pox and mumps when we lived there. Tommy was five years old and still sucked his thumb. It was so wrinkled it looked like the thumb of an old man. Daddy painted it with iodine. Tommy still sucked his thumb. Next, Daddy painted both thumbs with hot sauce. Still, he sucked his thumb. So Daddy bound both of Tommy's thumbs with strips of cloth. Tommy quit sucking his thumbs.

One day, Daddy and Johnny were going fishing at a nearby river; Tommy and I got to tag along. It was spring but still chilly enough that we wore our coats. Mine was a little red down-filled jacket. It helped save my life.

Johnny and Daddy walked further up river to fish, while me and Tommy played along the river's bank. We would roll down the bank to the river's edge, where a large, aged oak tree would break our roll, keeping us from rolling into the river.

We'd take turns, then scramble back up the bank laughing. Daddy had told us to stop but as soon as he was out of view, I went again!

This time I missed the tree and went rolling right into the river. Grabbing washed-out tree roots, I held tight but shock from the icy, cold water took my voice. The water was deep, with a swift current. I looked up to see Tommy's face was pale and stricken with fear. I could

8

make only feeble "peep" noises. Tommy could make none at all. Time seemed to have stopped until Daddy's arm reached down and I was yanked from the river's jaws. I was sent home with the promise of a whipping. Soaking, dripping wet, I ran all the way home more afraid of the promised whipping than the river.

Tommy's whippings became more frequent and intense as he grew older. Four-foot-long green switches increased from 2 and 3, to 4, and 5, then 6, and 7. Torture was added to the whippings by making Tommy cut his own switches.

If they weren't a satisfactory thickness and length, extra ones would be added to the total and Tommy sent back outside to start over. Another torture tactic was sending him to his room to wait for the whipping to come.

At the end of these whippings, the floor of his room would be littered by the broken pieces of switches. Daddy would emerge from the room wiping sweat from his forehead. Tommy's buttocks and the back of his legs would literally be blackened.

We were both nervous nail-biters and suffered from hangnails, but Tommy was also a bed-wetter. The more he peed his bed, the more he was whipped. Daddy's twisted mind was convinced Tommy was doing it out of defiance.

Sometime during the early seventies, actor/producer Michael Landon produced a movie about an Olympic runner. In the movie, a young boy began running home after school every day so he could take down his soiled bed sheets. Hung from their balcony like flags, his mother tried to shame her son from being a bed-wetter.

After the movie, Michael Landon delivered a message to viewers that many children's bodies grow faster than their bladder, which isn't developed enough to have control, a condition that corrects itself with time and growth.

Tommy outgrew bed-wetting but not soon enough. His beatings were sometimes daily. Bed-wetting was only one of the reasons he was beaten. He was also slapped off his feet, sometimes for no better reason than Daddy didn't like "the way" Tommy looked at him.

Only two of Tommy's school pictures were purchased during his eleven years of school. Daddy had told Momma not to buy any more of his pictures after the second grade. Sadly, our family album had only two of his school pictures and some snapshots sent by relatives. Tommy grew up to be a handsome man on the outside but on the inside he seemed to stay the same little boy wearing freckles and overalls.

Hunger was no stranger to Tommy. He was well acquainted with hunger long before he was homeless. We were skinny kids. Many times we were hungry because there was no food in our home. Daddy didn't kill himself to provide for us and he wouldn't "shame" himself by resorting to welfare, so we often went hungry.

This led to a lot of bad behavior from me. I began to steal other kid's lunches. During my fourth grade school year we had moved from West Virginia to California. We were living in a duplex apartment in Tracy, close enough to walk to a major grocery store. I began making trips to the store to steal a snack pie that I'd eat on my way home.

I taught Tommy the art of pie theft. Unfortunately, I didn't impress the importance of exiting out a side door enough to him. It wasn't long before he was caught stealing candy at the checkout isle. What was he thinking? WOE!

He received the grand prize: a free ride home in a police car. Walking home the closer I got to our front door, the louder I could hear my name being repeated by Tommy. "Darla told me to!" he sang like a canary!

We both got a beating. The good side was since we lived in a city, there was a shortage of green switches. So Daddy used his backup, the belt. At first I thought, "Lucky me!" Because while Daddy was in one room beating Tommy, Momma was in another beating me. All my thoughts of being blessed soon vanished, when to my horror they changed rooms like it was a square dance, dosey doe!

Needless to say, Tommy and I were mad at each other for a while. I quit stealing at the store and went back to kids' school lunches. I never recruited Tommy in any more of my theft. Daddy threatened to cut off my hand if I ever stole again so I was very careful and always ate all the evidence.

Give us this day our daily bread, Amen.

Left: Tommy~ age 5, Johnny~ age 9, Neal (cousin from Florida), Right: Darla~ age 6 ♡ and Mark~ age 2

Chapter 3

Despair

Our car trips across country were very tiresome. We got to see America's mountains, valleys, and deserts but the drive seemed endless. Several times while driving, Daddy dozed off and Momma screamed him awake. The drive would take a week.

Crossing the desert was the worst. Heat waves rose from the road pavement and hovered. Scenery never changed except for occasional jackrabbits darting across the road.

Our bodies felt cramped and we longed to stretch our legs. It was a rite of passage for the elder kids to sit by a door. Johnny and me always claimed our seat by a window. Tommy was always stuck in the middle. This worked out well because if we were put side by side, Johnny and I would fight.

Tommy would fall asleep and lay across my lap, then I would also fall asleep and lay on top of him. When we woke up we'd have slobber spots on each other.

We had made the trip when I was five and on that trip Momma kept getting sick into Dixie cups the entire trip. By the time we got to Virginia she had to be hospitalized. When we picked her up, she carried a little bundle in her arms. Weighing the same as a five-pound bag of sugar, and just as sweet, was our new baby brother, Mark. Now he was five years old and we were making the same trip back from California.

It was spring and school was still in progress. We had missed about four weeks of the school year from moving and resettling. Travel sore we bunked with relatives until we got our own place. Bunker Hill, West Virginia, would be our home for the next two years.

I was still in the fourth grade. When Momma tried leaving me in my new class at school, I broke down crying. Grabbing fistfulls of her skirt, I buried my face into her. Crying, I begged her not to leave me there. She did anyway.

We would get to attend this school long enough to get to know all our classmates' names. The teachers and students thought we were awesome because we had come from California. Most of them had never been out of West Virginia. I just wanted what they had: one place to call home and lifetime friends ... roots. We were tired of always being the new kids at school, weary of moving, and longed for normal lives.

The next two years we would suffer many hard times. Cold winters, no plumbing, and hunger would squeeze us to the brink of starvation. Daddy would work here and there some, then be out of work for long periods of time. He would sell a car, then be out of work the remainder of that year. Several times our electric was shut off.

We almost lost our little brother Mark to double pneumonia during a hard winter. Momma temporally got employment in a canning factory while Daddy "looked" for work.

These were the bleakest of days. Sometimes Daddy would sell something and we'd get groceries, but the food wouldn't last long and hunger returned.

Several times Momma argued with Daddy about letting us go to school where at least we'd get our lunch. He wanted to keep us home rather than send us to school hungry. At night my sleep was tormented by dreams of chocolate cake so real I could taste it. Tommy and I both worked in the school cafeteria washing lunch trays. We liked it, and it got us out of class early. Several other classmates worked for their lunch too.

Mark had been playing in Johnny's room one day with matches and a candle. After lighting the candle, he had leaned over to put the matches back when the flame caught his wool sweater on fire.

By the time he came running down the stairs his chest was engulfed in flames. We had never been taught to "STOP," "DROP," and "ROLL" in school. I screamed and froze. Tommy ran to get a bucket of water but by the time he returned, Momma had smothered out the fire with her hands.

The fire had burned through Mark's sweater, shirt, and undershirt. The center of his chest was badly burned. Momma had no car, we had no phone, and Daddy was in Maryland.

It took everything Mark's little body had to fight off infection.

His immune system was so stressed that later he got pneumonia in both lungs. We almost lost him twice that winter.

Daddy was in Maryland (working!) and Mark lay deathly ill. Momma had gone to use a neighbor's phone leaving me to watch over Mark. His fever was so high he couldn't even keep water down. Momma told me not to let him swallow his tongue if he went into convulsions. I was so scared, time crawled at a snail's pace until she returned.

Late that night, Daddy came home. Because I had let Tommy and Mark play outside in the snow when I had babysat them one no-school day, he blamed me for Mark's pneumonia. Tears rolled down my cheeks, falling to the floor while Daddy cussed and threatened me.

The shadow of death was over Mark and we knelt in the valley of despair united in prayer, begging God to spare his life.

Early the next morning Daddy and Momma wrapped Mark in blankets and headed for the hospital. Snow kept falling without mercy, but the old Falcon station wagon made the trip there and back home.

Mark was kept at the hospital where all the nurses fell in love with him. Never having had antibiotics made the penicillin work like a miracle drug. In only two days he was back home and feeling better. In no time at all he was back to normal, which was having his little head stuck between the stair banisters while Daddy and Momma worked hard at freeing him!

Mark's teacher sent Daddy and Momma home a note saying he just wasn't physically up to attending school and to go ahead and keep him home until the next school year.

Even though we should have been only a year apart in grade, Tommy had trouble in school and had failed twice. The end of the school year I was passed to the seventh grade and Tommy to the fifth. As summer began so also did my job of babysitting full time Becky, Mark, and Tommy.

Daddy, Momma, and Johnny had all gotten jobs in Bethesda, Maryland. They would leave Bunker Hill, West Virginia, at 4 a.m. and return at 7 p.m. five days a week.

Momma worked in a bank while Daddy and Johnny worked at a builder's supply company. Daddy was hired as manager, so he worked Johnny like a mule. He said he didn't want the other employees to complain he was easy on him because he was the boss's son. Unloading trucks filled with fifty-pound bags of cement all day was the price Johnny paid for it. He did a grown man's work at the age of fourteen.

Before school started we moved to Long Beach, Maryland. Momma got another job at a bank closer to home. Daddy also changed jobs, to an oil company near Andrews Air Force Base.

Our rented house was small but close enough to see the beach from it. For the next five and half years both our parents were employed. We would move two more times before I graduated from high school but we stayed in the same county attending the same schools.

Johnny would never work under Daddy again. He always managed to have a job so that he wouldn't have to.

We would enjoy a time of bounty. Food! A lit-up Christmas tree with presents beneath it! Best of all ... indoor plumbing, hot and cold!

Daddy's rage and abuse would remind us that we would never have normal lives. Security and peace would always be missing from under our roof. Tommy's beatings would increase and Daddy's temper would be like a hissing cobra, ready to strike without warning.

Momma worked full time and we all had chores to do. Mine were babysitting, housework, and washing the dishes. I was relieved not to have to do any cooking. Daddy was real picky about what Momma put on our table.

Supper always began with all heads bowed as Daddy said the blessing. But if her cooking didn't please him, as soon as "Amen" was out of his mouth he'd begin harassing Momma with insults, calling our supper "slop" and saying it wasn't fit for dogs or pigs. He constantly called her "the Saltless Wonder." The only resemblance to a pig at our table were Daddy's manners. After having been to the brink of starvation, we kids were grateful for our daily bread.

Johnny had gotten his driver's license at fifteen years old. With a car payment to make he was employed after school and weekends. He was rarely at home. Tall and broad-shouldered, with handsome James Dean rugged looks, we viewed him as an adult.

He also sparkled with a personality that drew people to him.

His hair was a thick, wavy brown with a bright auburn red birthmark the size of a silver dollar. If that wasn't unique enough, Mark's raven-black hair had the same size birthmark, except his was a pale blond. Everyone marveled over their birthmarks.

When he was young, Tommy's hair color was blond. As he grew older it darkened to a light brown. He didn't have a birthmark like his brothers. In Daddy's twisted mind it was an omen from God that Tommy wasn't his son. The unmarked son became marked from birth as the black sheep.

Depending on his mood, good, bad or ugly, we'd be beaten for the smallest thing. I was the official dishwasher and once I had forgotten to wash Daddy's coffee pot. I was beaten until I felt dizzy afterwards.

I never understood how Tommy endured the whippings he got. While he was being whipped, I would pray, never taking my eyes off the closed door. With my heart pounding, I'd wait for it to end, waiting for the door to open and Tommy to walk out. I lived in fear that one day, he wouldn't.

During the weekdays breakfast dishes were washed after I got home from school. Once a tiny speck of dried egg on his fork sent Daddy into a rage that ended in my having to wash all the silverware and dishes in the kitchen, both clean and dirty.

Daddy was a blasphemous man, often shouting to us, "I'm the great I AM in this house!" He ruled over us with all the tyranny, threats, abuse, and fear of Hitler's SS. We knew he wasn't God but we did fear he was the devil.

Deliver us from evil, Amen.

Chapter 4
Peace

I was six and Tommy four and a half years old when our family separated because we had no money for rent, food, or electric. Johnny and Tommy went to live with Daddy's older brother, our Uncle Bill, and his wife, Aunt Jean, in West Virginia. I was taken to Maryland and left with Momma's sister, our Aunt Charlotte, and her husband, Uncle Eddie. Mark was two years old and I don't remember who kept him.

I was so homesick for my family I cried every night into my pillow. My aunt and uncle were good to me, but I wanted to be with my own family. Tommy and I had bonded and we were pals. I couldn't understand why my parents didn't come and get me. Where were they? Where was Tommy? Didn't they want me anymore? What did I do wrong?

The separation lasted about seven months until Daddy and Momma, both employed, had saved enough money to get us a house in the country. After we were all reunited under one roof, Daddy quit working. Soon after that our house caught fire and burned while we were away on a visit to relatives. It was the first of two of our homes to be lost by fire.

Uncle Bill was a tall, wide-shouldered man built like a gladiator, slow to anger but not a man you would want angry at you! He lived a simple, humble life.

Wearing bib overalls and a smile that lifted up at the corners of his mouth is the way I'll always remember him. He loved to hunt, go to the races, music, and Aunt Jean.

He gave a guitar to Johnny and taught him some chords. Johnny amazed him at how fast he learned and how well he played. He also gave Johnny a man he could respect. I was given something too. I saw a man who both loved and respected his wife, never raising his voice to her. I had never seen such love and respect between a husband and wife. They were like a clear, cool drink of water to my heart. I knew there were good men in this world, and Uncle Bill was one of them.

Sadly, he died shortly after we moved from Bunker Hill, West Virginia, to Maryland. His death left an emptiness in all our lives, but Johnny's heart was shattered.

Tommy idolized Johnny and desperately wanted to be like him: tall, strong, well-liked, and courageous. Sadly, Daddy had poisoned his mind against ever believing he already had any of those very qualities that he could only see in others. So he stood in the shadows of giants, looking up and dreaming of someday being a mighty oak too.

Daddy had a third companion to complete his controlling and abusive personality ... racism. We grew up hearing "Coon, Wop, Dago, Jap, Chink, Jew, Spick," and his favorite ... "nigger."

In my fifth grade class there was one student who was African American. Being the new kid, I had latched onto her. She had a big smile that brightened the room and a sweet, kind demeanor that drew me to her.

Her name was Ethel and I couldn't pronounce it correctly, which resulted in my calling her "Esell." One day at recess I got mad and called her the "N" word. She told our teacher and when he asked me if I had, I lied and said, "No!" We were dismissed to return to our seats and no more was said concerning the matter.

One look at Ethel's face and I saw the hurt and injustice of being treated unequal. I felt shame and guilt. She had always been so nice to me and I had returned her kindness with a bad name, crowning it with a lie.

I felt certain our teacher knew this and slighted Ethel by dismissing the matter so easily. I apologized to Ethel but I never forgot our teacher's part in the offense toward her.

One Saturday when Daddy wasn't home, Ethel and another classmate invited me to walk with them to Ethel's house. I got to meet Ethel's momma and see her new baby brother. I could see Ethel was just as full of love and pride for her baby brother as I was of mine, Mark.

Even after we moved away and I never saw Ethel again, I kept her with me inside my heart.

Every time Daddy tried to poison my mind with his racism, I saw Ethel's smiling face. You never know how far a small kindness will go in another's life.

April 3, 1968, we were living in Huntingtown, Maryland, when Dr. Martin Luther King, Jr. was assassinated. I was in the eighth grade. As the news footage ran across our television, Daddy's voice thundered, "About time somebody shot that damn nigger!" and "They ought to give the shooter a medal!"

Dr. King's dream of brotherhood between the races was a divine rhythm that beat from his heart's desire. A desire united with God for peace on earth and goodwill toward all mankind.

The chambers of Daddy's heart were filled with bigotry's poison. He could only turn a deaf ear to profound words, while spewing profanity from his own lips. His heart embraced KKK and his mouth foamed with its madness.

He also hated Robert Kennedy because he had worked with Dr. King on civil rights for black Americans. Daddy referred to him as a "nigger lover S.O.B."

Daddy controlled our lives but he couldn't indoctrinate our hearts and minds with his poison. It was our one freedom he didn't have any power over…the freedom to choose! Dr. King and Robert Kennedy both have a special place in Heaven I believe. Their hearts were special enough to devote themselves to trying to make a better world for us all to live in together. God's eyes search the world for people like them. Their lives in this world were brief, but they left it a better one than it was when they were born into it.

Their hearts were made of special dust, for a special time in history. A time of human rights.

Blessed are the peacemakers: For they shall be called the children of God.

Matthew 5:9

Chapter 5

Mercy

Daddy was as controlling as he was abusive. When we got a phone in our home, he installed a second one. Every call was listened in on by him. When the phone rang, he would tell us to wait until he got to the second one, then yell when it was O.K. to pick up the receiver. He never hid the fact that all our calls were being listened in on by him. Of course the caller on the other end never knew this.

We weren't allowed to ask Momma's permission for anything. If we did it sent Daddy into one of his, "I'm the great I AM in this house!" rages. We lived like scared little mice not daring to provoke his wrath. Except Johnny, who was made of stronger dust than us.

We were never encouraged to join after-school activities. When he was fourteen, Johnny had joined the school football team. One day after school he and three teammates were outside passing a football back and forth.

Daddy yelled for Johnny to come inside. We all heard anger in his voice. As soon as he was inside, enraged Daddy hit him in the face, knocking him to the floor, and giving him a bad nosebleed. His rage was over one of the boys outside being African American. Johnny quit the football team the next day at school.

As soon as he got a car and job we rarely saw Johnny.

I always thought he worked to escape being at home around Daddy. He couldn't bear being controlled by a man he'd lost respect for long ago. His was an independent spirit. By the age of sixteen he had a taste for more than just independence … alcohol. He never drank in our home or our presence, but his new habit would become a lifetime one.

Daddy never drank, not even a beer. He held a tight grip on control, not letting loose of even an ounce of it. All of the abuse we suffered came from him, not an empty bottle.

An expoliceman and avid hunter, Daddy had a large collection of guns by the time I was in high school.

Many times I was sure he would cross the line of sanity to insanity and shoot us all, especially when his anger was zeroed in on Momma.

One night his threats to shoot her were so loud and filled with anger, I went to bed fully dressed, including my shoes. I thought if I heard any shots fired I could at least take my little sister and escape out our bedroom window.

Sleep finally rescued me from the hell and turmoil and daybreak brought comfort when I was awakened by Momma for school.

After Johnny joined the army, an ocean and a war separated us from him, so we mice were on our own. At times I thought he was safer where he was than we were.

There had been another night of Daddy's abuse to Momma. At the time Johnny was sixteen and home. Daddy had been yelling and cussing her all day. As his threats escalated, Tommy and I stood trembling and biting our fingernails down to the wick. By this time we were nervous wrecks.

From upstairs Momma started screaming and Johnny bolted to Daddy's deer rifle. A jammed bullet in its chamber was all that kept Daddy from being shot that night.

After that Daddy knew Johnny was a force of his own, a force he didn't want to unleash. Johnny had taken ownership of himself and never again would he be bullied or controlled. We stood in awe of his courage. We were still mice but he was a young lion!

Johnny could never understand why Daddy treated us so unjustly, why he had to bully his wife and kids to feel like a big man. Still he asks, "Why?"

And ye fathers provoke not your children to wrath.

Ephesians 6:4

Chapter 6
Humility

Tommy's sweet tooth always got him into trouble. When he was four years old, Momma chased him from the kitchen outside with her broom. He'd spilt the sugar bowl all over her wet, freshly scrubbed floor. When she saw the broken bowl and sticky mess, she was mad as a hornet!

The sight of her with the broom in her hand made me and Johnny run too! Sugar was as much a luxury in our house as gold dust. We knew she meant business and that the broom was no longer a cleaning tool but her choice of weapon.

The sight of us all running like mice from a cat made her laugh too hard to catch anything but the dust from our feet! Johnny thought she was after him, while I was sure it was me she was after. Only Tommy knew why he ran. Her only chance of catching any of us was if she rode her broom.

There was another time Tommy's sweet tooth almost got him killed....

After we moved from Long Beach to Huntingtown, Maryland, we stayed in the same school zone. I was going into the eighth grade, Tommy sixth, Mark third, Becky first, and Johnny tenth.

Our two-story rented house sat on a hilltop. At the bottom of our hill sat a gas station/grocery store owned by our landlord. Johnny worked there after school and weekends.

One Saturday Tommy walked to the store to buy some candy. When he stepped into the store a shotgun was shoved in his face. The store was being robbed. Johnny told them not to hurt him, that he was only a kid. They were all made to lay face down in a back stockroom, then the robbers fled.

Later Daddy got the brilliant idea to connect an alarm from our house to the store. A button could be pushed from the store that set off a very loud ringing bell in our house.

We were given instructions that if it went off we were to: 1. Go outside, walk toward the store. 2. Wait to see if anyone came out to tell us if it was a false alarm. 3. If no one came out and told us it was a false alarm, we were to go back to our house and call the police. Simple as that. We should have known we would be tested.

When the alarm started ringing Momma told Tommy to go check it out. Still traumatized from the first robbery, he wasn't having anything to do with a second one.

Next she told me to go. Not even in her dreams was she going to get me past our door frame. It wasn't happening! That left only Mark and Becky. Their eyes were swelled open like deer caught in headlights and shaking their heads, Noooo!

We were still arguing about it when the door slammed shut and in walked Daddy wearing a disgusted look on his face.

He yelled at us mice and cussed before disconnecting the alarm.

Tommy's sweet tooth starved for a year and Johnny got a new job.

That same summer Tommy and Mark made an alliance. I was fourteen and spent more time looking in the mirror than at what the kids were up to. Mark and Tommy had been busy building forts, digging tunnels, and spying on me. They bonded.

One day Mark had an attitude and smart mouth with me. So I took Tommy aside and told him of a plan I had to beat the stuffing out of Mark by making it appear to be a game we were "playing." This way if I "accidentally" hurt him, I wouldn't get into trouble. I planned to just hurt him enough to make him humble.

The plan was, I would make a square in the dirt which would be our "boxing ring," the boxers being Mark and me. All was going well, although I did catch Tommy and Mark whispering and looking at me.

If I hadn't been so clueless I wouldn't have been so quick to shake off my doubts. I set all the rules which amounted to when I said, "Ding! Ding! Ding!" we would stop boxing and each go to our corners. O.K? O.K.

Trouble was, their alliance wasn't the only thing I had overlooked that summer. When the fight began, instead of me pounding the liver out of Mark, he was knocking me brainless in round one!

I was being savagely attacked by a fierce little "Rocky" while I was a "Raggedy Ann." My hairbrush was the only thing I'd been lifting.

I began screaming, "Ding! Ding! Ding!" only to discover Mark was a little rule-breaker! And to my horror Tommy was rolling on the ground, laughing so hard he was crying! This only inspired Mark to commence fiercer. Woe!

Realizing I had lost "face" and all control over them, I ran into the house and up the stairs with Mark hot on my heels. He wasn't willing to let his moment of glory end so soon.

Midway up the stairs I turned on the landing where a second battle ensued. I was fighting now to regain any authority I could reclaim. I managed to rip Mark's shirt and break his watchband, mostly from defending myself from his fist. Clearly he was the victor. As loser, I did the only thing left … I ran to my room cussing them both and crying!

After Daddy got home and we were all gathered at the supper table eating, I was asked if the kids were good. Both Mark and Tommy stopped chewing their food. Their eyes plastered on me. It was a rare golden moment where time stopped and just hung in midair above them, until I weakly answered, "Yeah, they were good." Needless to say they ran amuck the rest of that summer, even Becky, the little one!

Tommy and Mark's bond grew stronger and tighter over the years. They hunted the Ozarks of Missouri and the mountains of West Virginia. They worked side by side in the fields of South Carolina, until like mine, Mark's childhood memories are filled with Tommy.

It was to our father's shame that he never saw the dear son he had in Tommy, or how much a part of our family and hearts he was to the rest of us. Without Tommy our family wasn't whole or complete. It was a broken circle. He had his place in our hearts and no one could take that away, not even Daddy.

When we were growing up, "nigger" was a word we heard all too often in our home. It was the nickname Daddy called our mother. We kids were forbidden to use it but when Daddy wasn't around and we were fighting, it was our name of choice to call each other. Until Momma put a bar of ivory soap in our mouths and raked it across our teeth.

Tommy and I never referred to each other by that name again. Too bad she couldn't have done the same to Daddy's mouth!

Teach your children the ways you would have them go.

Proverbs 22:6

Chapter 7

Grace

The line drawn for us to walk went beyond strict. Our childhood was a tight balancing act and if we faltered there was no grace. When Daddy entered the room our brain automatically shifted to defense mode, our heart rates increased, our bodies tensed, and silence filled the room.

If his voice was raised with our name, we'd swallow our heart, where it raced in the pit of our stomach. His tactics of terror and abuse cost him a price though. He never really got to know us. Under his condemnation we shrank deep into ourselves, surviving by staying hidden there. We weren't free to speak our minds or dare to disagree. We had no voice, just silence.

Time was on our side but its slow tick-tock wasn't much comfort. Johnny said Army boot camp was a piece of cake after being raised by Daddy.

Even though Tommy repeatedly ran away, no help came for him. When he was seen by a psychologist, Momma was told there was nothing wrong with him but his father had a problem.

Since the garden of Eden, evil has always worn a mask. Daddy masked his evil very carefully. He always moved us to secluded houses keeping us far enough away from neighbors so they couldn't witness his abuse.

The move from West Virginia to Maryland was a major step up the ladder from poverty to middle class. After two years of renting, our parents became homeowners. Our new home was in Port Republic, Maryland, within walking distance to the beach of Scientist Cliffs. The house was a contractor built, ranch style with a full basement.

Momma now had a new washer and dryer, no longer having to use the old wringer washer or laundromats. Our basement had double french doors, a bar, bathroom, family room, and a large bedroom.

Upstairs there were two bedrooms, living room, kitchen, and bathroom. The floors were varnished hardwood upstairs and tiled downstairs. Heated by oil, there would be no more cold nights. Water shortage would never be a problem because we had an artesian well. Our new home sat secluded on several acres well off the road.

Because our home was so secluded with no one there during the day, we had three full-grown german shepherd guard dogs: Cougar, a brown and tan male, Cheetah, a silver and black female with papers, and Chief, son of Cougar and Cheetah. Even when a rash of break-ins occurred all around the beach, our home was never broken into.

We would get to call this "home" for the next four years, until Daddy quit his job, sold our home, and moved to Clio, South Carolina. He would never be employed again.

Momma had just been promoted to head teller of the bank's new branch. She had to quit her job.

In Clio, South Carolina, a fifty-acre farm with house and barn were bought. Daddy was going to be a farmer. It lasted two years then the farm was sold. A 160-acre ranch was bought in Squires, Missouri.

Daddy was a cattle rancher for eight months. The ranch was sold and two houses on a piece of property were bought in West Virginia. It was "U-Haul" time again.

While we were living in South Carolina our german shepherd Cheetah wounded Daddy's pet kitten. He took her into the woods that night, making Tommy shine a flashlight on her while he shot her. She had been a part of our family since she was a four-month-old puppy, seven years. It always bothered Tommy that he had been a part of her execution.

Cheetah had been beaten mercilessly and kicked many times by Daddy and yet she would have given her life protecting his. He knew this and still took her life in a moment of anger. His temper never mellowed with age, it grew thinner and sharper, like a razor's edge.

Tommy had quit school and was working at a John Deere tractor company. His paycheck was given to Daddy and any time off he spent working on the farm. Even though Daddy's temper would flare up and Tommy get slapped and cussed, he would remain a willing servant until Daddy died in 1978. Now he knows who the true "GREAT I AM" is!

Daddy had chronic ingrown toenails so he made Tommy sit on the floor with a pair of nail clippers working on his toes for hours. He also liked his head scratched, so another one of us would be behind his chair scratching his head.

No matter where we lived, Momma made our house a home. It wasn't just her domestic touches that made it a bearable place to be, but her presence in it.

A light shined from her soul and all the ugly words and hatred that came from Daddy couldn't dim that light. She was young at heart, made us laugh, and taught us to pray. Her gentle spirit balanced the scales with her love being equal to the violence and abuse of Daddy.

His wrath and abuse were on her many times. Several times she left, but he would track her down each time. I saw the same fear in her eyes that was in our own. She was as helpless against him as her children were.

When she spoke up for Tommy, it made his life harder. Daddy would pick on him, calling him "Momma's little titty baby."

In one of their last conversations over the phone, Momma teased Tommy, telling him she was going to run away and come live with him. She asked him if she were to panhandle, if he thought people would give money to her too?

The thought of Momma panhandling tickled Tommy, making him laugh so hard he forgot all his worries and troubles even if it was just for a few minutes.

She had a special way of making burdens seem lighter. That was the gift she gave to us all. Her hands smoothed away the wrinkles from our forehead.

Her children arise up and call her blessed.
Proverbs 31:28

Chapter 8

His

During our childhood years many abuses were inflicted on us. Both Johnny and Tommy turned to alcohol. Tommy's addiction became chronic.

During 1979 or '80, Tommy was working at an oil drilling refinery in Louisiana close to the border of Texas. There he met and fell in love with an Italian girl from Dallas.

Her parents owned a restaurant, which was most likely a business cover for another ... the mob. Her father persuaded her to marry a policeman, most likely on the mob's payroll.

I'm not sure if she married the policeman to protect her unborn baby, Tommy, or both. I do know Tommy believed the daughter she gave birth to was his. Around this same time Tommy testified before a grand jury concerning a mob hit man. He was tortured and warned by the mob that if he was ever found in Dallas again he would be a dead man.

Tommy told me he was in the federal witness protection program, which explains why he had four different Social Security numbers.

The U.S. Department of Justice will neither confirm nor deny his participation in the witness security program.

Although homeless, Tommy risked his life and did more against organized crime than most 9 to 5 working citizens. He was viewed by society as just another homeless transient. He liked to refer to himself as a street warrior. I think of him as he is now, a warrior for Christ!

When he was just a little boy and asked what he wanted to be when he grew up, he answered, "a policeman." Tommy had done some undercover work with the drug task force which led to a large drug bust during the late seventies in West Virginia.

By the time he was twenty years old he was a sharpshooter. One hunting season he bagged a trophy buck with a ten-point rack. With a single bullet, he shot it right between the eyes. One look at the huge buck and Daddy's green eyes turned a shade greener.

Tommy's death certificate states "Transient" and "Chronic alcoholism" but he was so much more than a homeless drunkard. Most of all he was an abused child who couldn't fit into life as an adult because he was beaten into too many little pieces that none of us could fit them back together for him.

Many survive child abuse and go on to live productive lives. But the pain one heart can bear sometimes breaks another's. Tommy's was the one that broke.

The battle against evil begins in the hearts of mankind. With his free will Tommy choose to put his own life in danger.

Because we were raising children of our own, Mark, Becky, and I enforced a policy of no alcohol or drugs in our homes. It was a rule Tommy couldn't keep. Each time he was taken in by a family member, he would stay sober maybe two months then leave or get intoxicated. Alcohol transformed him into a belligerent, foul-mouthed vessel. Rage and anger he was never able to express flooded out of the Pandora's box in fits of violence and death threats.

Tommy will always be special to me. His heart was never put into Pandora's box but instead into Jesus' hands. Instead of hating Daddy, he chose to love and forgive him. The rhythm of his heartbeat was a divine one. Cold, sickness, hunger, and pain were what he knew most in this world.

Lazarus and Tommy had much in common. One begged for crumbs of food, the other for crumbs of love and mercy. Both of them starved, now they both dwell in Heaven!

How many Tommies are in the process of being beaten down and whipped into future broken people destined to roam the streets?

When compassion was replaced by manifest destiny, the American Indian people suffered, leaving history a trail of tears. When the South's greed replaced compassion, African Americans were dehumanized and enslaved. When a nation's compassion is replaced by apathy, homeless people die on it's streets. There are over 700,000 homeless people in America as I write this. "Why?"

Cities try to rid themselves of the homeless like unwanted weeds in their rose gardens. Blankets are confiscated from the homeless by city police. Sleeping homeless are awakened and harassed to move on. Tommy would argue that a park bench was property of the public, not private. It was an argument he always lost.

Many homeless people die every winter from frostbite, hypothermia, and pneumonia. Tommy spent several winters homeless in Washington, D.C., and Texas. He once witnessed a fight over placement in a soup line. One stabbed the other to death over a meal. One hot meal can be the difference between freezing to death or living to see tomorrow.

Since the homeless don't vote, they seem to have lost all their constitutional rights. Although that's nothing new, our lawmakers move like slugs when protecting children's rights also. (Gee, could it be because they don't vote either?)

Are we living in a nation where only voters have rights? I don't believe that's what the framers of our constitution had in mind when they wrote it. Our constitution came from the hearts and minds of people trying to secure justice, equality, and freedom for all! Even the homeless and children who don't vote.

The strong were put here to protect the weak. When we stand before God and are asked how did we care for His little ones, what will we answer?

Some ask, "Why?" of God. I ask, "Why?" of humanity.

Little ones to Him belong.

From song, "Jesus Loves Me"
By William B. Bradbury

Chapter 9

Rest

Sometime around the year 2000 while Tommy was sitting on a street curb, a bread delivery truck ran over the curb, pinning him beneath the truck. I don't know the full extent of what his injuries were, except he had to have surgery on his foot and pins were used to repair it. Afterwards he walked with a pronounced limp. He had a lawsuit in progress.

Shortly before he died, while attending the Children of The Shepherd Church in Hollywood, Tommy requested the hymn "Just As I Am" and in humility walked to the altar, where he knelt down and received God's salvation. A great multitude of angels rejoiced that very instant.

Satan's lip twisted with defeat and Jesus smiled in victory!

Early the morning of September 15, 2005, Tommy called to talk to Momma. He said he'd been beaten up that night. One eye was swollen shut from having been kicked in it and his stomach hurt. Momma begged him to go to an emergency room. It was the last time she would talk to him.

That evening Tommy walked into the Hollywood Presbyterian Medical Center's emergency room, said his stomach hurt, then dropped dead.

Before his body fell to the floor, an angel reached out a hand, taking Tommy to Heaven where Jesus and a great host of His angels were waiting for him. God's gates swung open welcoming Tommy forever home.

Daddy was used as a wicked instrument by Satan trying to corrupt Tommy's heart with hatred. As harsh as his treatment from Daddy was, he never let it harden his heart. Keeping his heart "few and far between" made him a beautiful gem to the Lord.

It doesn't matter who our earthly father is because there's a bigger, better place called Heaven and that's where the true Father of us all waits to welcome His children home.

Tommy is now called "Beloved!" He was treated as the least of us five kids in our home, but in God's house he's treated as the prince of a King of kings! Tommy endured and overcame evil. He was made of finer dust than most!

Blessed are the pure in heart: for they shall see God.
Matthew 5:8

Epilogue

Dressed in black velvet and wearing diamonds, the night sky sparkled with an ominous air of frost above the city lights. It promised to be a bitter cold night for both man and beast.

On one of America's streets a young homeless mother held her baby close. Her own body heat was all she could give her baby and there was very little to give. She knew they wouldn't make it through the night. Arctic winds and the chill factor would lower their body temperature until all life was frozen out of them.

She began to pray. She could see her breath as each one stung her lungs like thousands of sharp needles. Her words were mumbled by numbed lips. Involuntarily her body shook against the cold. Tears streamed down her cheeks falling as softly as each word ... "In Christ Jesus' name, Amen."

God heard her prayer and sent one of His new warriors, one who had known the cold and the streets. The span of his wings was eighteen feet, nine feet each wing.

Shadowy figures slinked deeper into the darkness, distancing themselves from him with angry hisses.

Standing behind her, he opened his wings to their full span. Gently as a dove he folded them around her and the child, blanketing them in a Heavenly warmth. She never saw him but her baby stirred, opened his eyes, and smiled before resuming sleep.

A dimmed daylight awakened the city to a tapestry of finely woven ice crystals left in the night's wake. The mother and her child both survived the coldest night of winter as if they had been wrapped in quilts of the finest down.

About the Author

Darla Kellar is a wife, mother of three and grandmother of three. She writes from her home in Independence, West Virginia. She is the founder of "The Remembering Tommy" foundation to benefit America's homeless.